AZERBAIJAN

AZERBAIJAN

A0002600381244

Prepared by
Geography Department

Lerner Publications Company
Minneapolis

THEN & NOW

Series editors: Mary M. Rodgers, Tom Streissguth,
  Colleen Sexton
Photo researcher: Bill Kauffmann
Designer: Zachary Marell

Our thanks to the following for their help in preparing
and checking the text of this book: Dr. Craig ZumBrun-
nen, Department of Geography, University of Washington;
Dr. Ron Wixman, Department of Geography, University of
Oregon.

Terms in **bold** appear in a glossary that starts on page 52.

Pronunciation Guide

glasnost	GLAZ-nost
Kyrgyzstan	keer-GEEZ-stan
mosque	MAHSK
muezzin	moo-EZ-in
Nagorno-Karabakh	neh-gawr-no—KAR-eh-bak
Nakhichevan	nak-ih-cheh-VAN
Shiite	SHEE-iyt
Tbilisi	teh-BILL-eh-see
Zoroastrianism	zor-uh-WAAS-tree-uh-nihz-um

LIBRARY OF CONGRESS CATALOGING-IN-PUBLICATION DATA

Azerbaijan / prepared by Geography Department, Lerner
  Publications Company.
      p. cm. — (Then & now)
    Includes index.
    Summary: Discusses the topography, location, ethnic
  mixture, history, economic activities, and future of the former
  Soviet republic of Azerbaijan.
    ISBN 0-8225-2810-X (lib. bdg.)
    1. Azerbaijan—Juvenile literature. [1. Azerbaijan.] I. Lerner
  Publications Company. Geography dept. II. Series: Then & Now
  DK692.23.A97 1992
  947'.91—dc20   92-24954
                                                      CIP
                                                       AC

Manufactured in the United States of America
1 2 3 4 5 6 98 97 96 95 94 93

Azeri girls rest on a swing near Mingechaur, a town in north central Azerbaijan.

"We will fight until we win."

Yussef Samadoglu
Azerbaijan Popular Front

In 1992, the Soviet Union would have celebrated the 75th anniversary of the revolution of 1917. During that revolt, political activists called **Communists** overthrew the czar (ruler) and the government of the **Russian Empire.** The revolution of 1917 was the first step in establishing the 15-member **Union of Soviet Socialist Republics (USSR).**

The Soviet Union stretched from eastern Europe across northern Asia and contained nearly 300 million people. Within this vast nation, the Communist government guaranteed housing, education, health care, and lifetime employment. Communist leaders told farmers and factory workers that Soviet citizens owned all property in common. The new nation quickly **industrialized,** meaning it built many new factories and upgraded existing ones. It also modernized and enlarged its farms. In addition, the USSR created a huge, well-equipped military force that allowed it to become one of the most powerful nations in the world.

In 1992, an ongoing ethnic conflict worsened in Nagorno-Karabakh —an Azeri territory with a majority population of Armenians. During lulls in the fighting, the citizens of Stepanakert, the region's major city, left their shelters in search of water, food, and other necessities.

An Azeri veteran (left) of World War II (1939–1945) shows off his medals in the ancient northern town of Sheki. During the Soviet era, a display (below) near Azerbaijan's border with Georgia carried emblems of the 15 Soviet republics.

By the early 1990s, the Soviet Union was in a period of rapid change and turmoil. The central government had mismanaged the economy, which was failing to provide goods. To control the various ethnic groups within the USSR, the Communists had long restricted many freedoms. People throughout the vast nation were dissatisfied.

In Azerbaijan and Armenia—two small, neighboring Soviet republics in the southwestern USSR—this discontent erupted in a violent ethnic conflict. A long-standing feud between the two republics resulted in the deaths of many Azeris (the people of Azerbaijan) and Armenians. To put down the unrest, the Soviet president Mikhail Gorbachev sent troops to occupy the Azeri capital of Baku. Despite this intervention, the violence continued.

Azerbaijan and Armenia, along with several other republics, began to seek independence from Soviet rule—a development that worried some old-style Communists. In August 1991, these conservative Communists tried to use Soviet military power to overthrow Gorbachev. Their effort failed and hastened the breakup of the USSR.

Gorbachev's willingness to interfere in the fight between Azerbaijan and Armenia had angered Azerbaijan's Communist leaders, who at first supported the coup. But the Popular Front—Azerbaijan's main pro-independence group—pressured the Azeri government to declare self-rule in September of 1991.

The ethnic conflict in Azerbaijan has intensified since the country gained independence. Guerrilla fighters on both sides shell villages and towns, and thousands of Azeris and Armenians have been killed or wounded. With a well-developed industrial sector and large oil resources, Azerbaijan may yet prosper if it can peacefully resolve its dispute with Armenia.

Young refugees from the war in Nagorno-Karabakh enjoy games, sunshine, and peace in southern Azerbaijan.

CHAPTER ONE

The Land and People of Azerbaijan

T he modern Republic of Azerbaijan is made up of the lands of the former Azerbaijan Soviet Socialist Republic. Part of southwestern Asia, Azerbaijan covers 33,400 square miles (86,600 square kilometers), an area that is slightly larger than Austria or than the state of Maine.

Several former Soviet republics border Azerbaijan. The Dagestan region of Russia, for example, lies to the north. To the west is Georgia, and to the southwest is Armenia. Georgia, Armenia, and Azerbaijan are sometimes called the **Transcaucasian republics,** after the Caucasus Mountains that stretch through their territories.

Most Azeris follow the Shiite sect of the Islamic religion. Here, a muezzin (crier) calls the faithful to prayer from the balcony of a mosque (house of worship).

West of Baku, the capital of Azerbaijan, the terrain is rugged and barren.

Iran (ancient Persia) sits south of Azerbaijan, and the oil-rich Caspian Sea—the world's largest inland saltwater lake—borders Azerbaijan to the east. Azerbaijan has roughly 300 miles (483 km) of valuable coastline along this sea. Baku, the capital, is one of the Caspian Sea's major ports.

Azerbaijan also has two unusual territorial features. Nakhichevan, a small piece of Azeri territory located southwest of Armenia, is cut off from the rest of Azerbaijan. Similarly, within Azerbaijan is Nagorno-Karabakh, a region with an Armenian majority but no physical connection to Armenia. Armenians and Azeris have fought over these two territories for many decades.

• The Lay of the Land •

Azerbaijan has a variety of landscapes. About 40 percent of the country consists of plains and lowlands. Another 10 percent is dominated by the Caucasus Mountains. The remaining half of the nation's territory is elevated flatland.

Most Azeris live in the lowlands and valleys of the Kura and Araks rivers of central and southern Azerbaijan. The Kura flows eastward from Georgia and empties into the Caspian Sea. The Araks, which forms Nakhichevan's border with Iran, begins in Turkey and travels to meet the Kura River near the Azeri town of Sabirabad. Both of these rivers irrigate the region's farmland.

Spurs of the Greater Caucasus Mountains extend into northern Azerbaijan. This range has many

Herders drive their sheep to winter pastures in Nakhichevan, the southern Azeri territory that borders Iran and Armenia.

peaks that exceed 14,000 feet (4,267 meters) in elevation. Mount Bazardyuze lies near the Russian border in northern Azerbaijan. At 14,698 feet (4,480 m) above sea level, this peak is the highest point in the country.

The Greater Caucasus nearly reach the shores of the Caspian Sea at the Apsheron Peninsula in eastern Azerbaijan. The peninsula occupies a strategic location along trade routes north to Russia and southwest to the Middle East. Oil wells, refining facilities, and assembly plants in the area have also helped to make the Apsheron Peninsula an important industrial hub.

In western Azerbaijan, the Lesser Caucasus Mountains run along the border with Armenia. Several peaks in the Lesser Caucasus reach heights of between 10,000 and 12,000 feet (3,048 and 3,658 m) above sea level. The Talysh Mountains are in the southwestern corner of Azerbaijan on the Iranian frontier.

• *Climate* •

Most of Azerbaijan is dry, receiving 6 to 10 inches (15 to 25 centimeters) of annual rainfall. The lowlands have mild winters but experience extremely hot summers, with temperatures frequently exceeding 100° F (38° C). In Baku, on the Apsheron Peninsula, average temperatures in January, the coldest month, are 39° F (4° C). In July, the hottest month, readings in the capital hover around 78° F (26° C). Baku also is hit by strong winds that blow off the Caspian Sea.

The weather in mountainous areas of Azerbaijan varies with altitude. Rainfall in the highland regions averages 40 inches (102 cm) per year. This heavy precipitation provides much of the water used to irrigate farms in the lowlands.

A father and son enjoy the waters of the Mingechaur Reservoir in central Azerbaijan. A dam built on the Kura River created the huge reservoir.

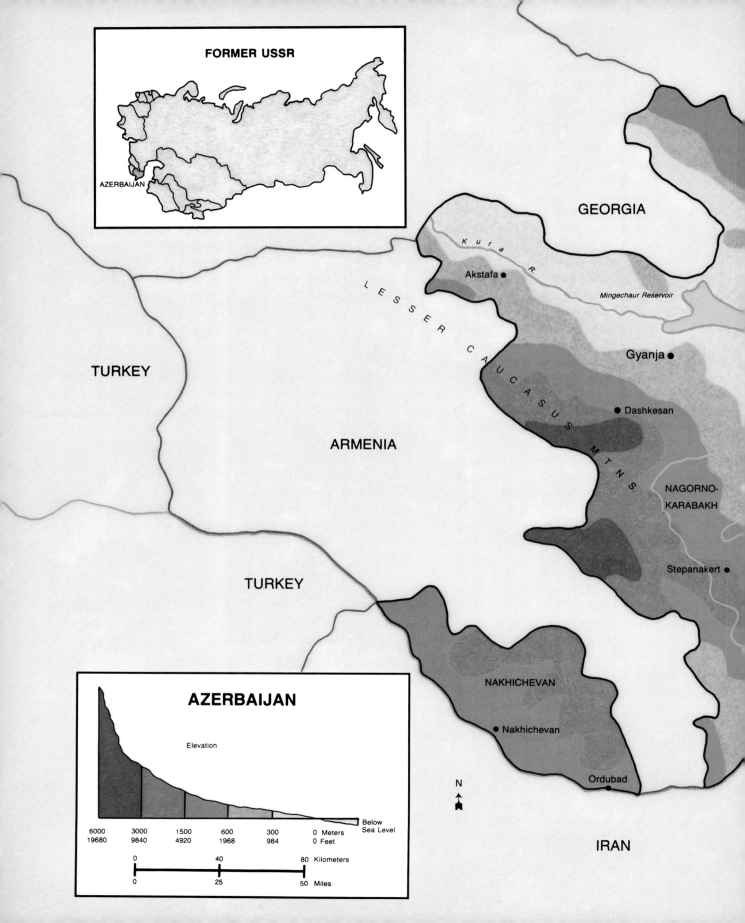

FORMER USSR

AZERBAIJAN

GEORGIA

Kura R.

Akstafa ●

Mingechaur Reservoir

TURKEY

L E S S E R   C A U C A S U S   M T N S.

Gyanja ●

● Dashkesan

ARMENIA

NAGORNO-
KARABAKH

TURKEY

Stepanakert ●

NAKHICHEVAN

● Nakhichevan

N

Ordubad
●

AZERBAIJAN

Elevation

| 6000 | 3000 | 1500 | 600 | 300 | 0 Meters | Below |
| 19680 | 9840 | 4920 | 1968 | 984 | 0 Feet | Sea Level |

| 0 | | 40 | | 80 Kilometers |
| 0 | | 25 | | 50 Miles |

IRAN

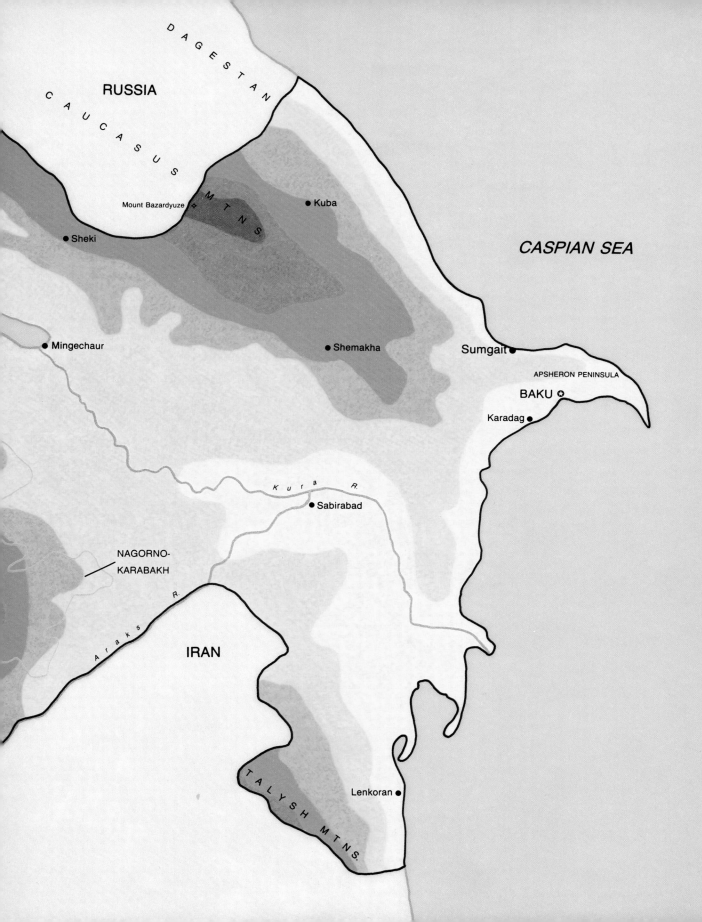

• Cities •

To find better jobs and educational opportunities, many rural Azeris have moved to the cities since the 1950s and 1960s. Fighting that broke out in 1988 between Armenians and Azeris brought refugees into some urban areas. Many Azeris living in Armenia also emigrated to Azerbaijan, mainly to Baku. Today, more than half of Azerbaijan's 7.1 million people live in cities.

Although Baku has a long history, it did not emerge as a modern capital until the late 19th century, when oil was discovered in the Caspian Sea. With 1.1 million residents, Baku is now the largest city in Azerbaijan. Factories in the capital produce oil equipment, ships, machinery, chemicals, tools, and textiles.

Baku was once under the control of Persian rulers called shahs. The city became part of the Russian Empire in the early 1800s. The castle district still contains ancient gates and narrow, twisting streets. These oldest parts of Baku are now obscured by new buildings, apartment complexes, and universities built in the early 20th century. Not far from Baku is a residential and industrial complex that rests on iron pilings sunk in the Caspian Sea.

With 274,000 inhabitants, Gyanja (called Kirovabad in the Soviet period) is Azerbaijan's second largest city and an important food-processing and

Buildings in old sections of Baku reflect the capital's past as an Islamic stronghold and trading center.

Cranes and oil wells dominate the harbor and bay of modern Baku.

Vendors offer flowers at a farmer's market in the city of Gyanja (formerly Kirovabad).

cotton center. Once a major Persian outpost, Gyanja boasts many architectural wonders dating as far back as the 11th century. The Persian shah Abbas I, for example, built the Dzhuma Mosque (an Islamic house of prayer) in 1603. A caravansary, or traveler's inn, still stands, as do parts of a 13th-century fortress.

Just to the north of Baku, on the Apsheron Peninsula, is Sumgait (population 235,000), the third largest city of Azerbaijan. Like Baku, Sumgait owes its existence to the discovery of oil and natural gas in the region. Violence between Azeris and Armenians in Sumgait broke out in 1988 and sparked ethnic clashes between the two groups that continued in the early 1990s.

• *Ethnic Groups and Languages* •

Many peoples have passed through and settled in Azerbaijan during the country's history. Each group has helped to shape Azeri culture. In the early 1990s, **ethnic Azeris** accounted for more than 80 percent of the nation's population. **Ethnic Russians**, who have a Slavic background, and **ethnic Armenians**—an ancient Christian people—together made up the largest ethnic minorities in Azerbaijan.

Although ethnic Armenians have lived in Azerbaijan since antiquity, their numbers soared in the early 1800s, when wars in their homeland caused Armenians to move elsewhere. Because of the ethnic strife that began in 1988, thousands of Armenians —as well as many Russians—have emigrated from

Many Azeri boys are fitness enthusiasts and spend hours racing, doing chin-ups, and learning new sports.

Azerbaijan. In addition, many Azeris have returned from Armenia. As a result, Azerbaijan is becoming more ethnically uniform.

Azerbaijan's earliest settlers—known as Caucasic people—were from the Caucasus area. Beginning about 3,500 years ago, peoples related to the Persians (modern Iranians) moved into the lowlands of Azerbaijan and intermarried with the Caucasic peoples. In the 11th century, Seljuk Turks invaded the area from central Asia. During the next several centuries, a process of **Turkization** took place, during which most of the people adopted Turkish culture.

The Seljuk Turks brought the Turkish language to Azerbaijan. Azeri, the language spoken by the

(Above) *Arabic words are carved above the doorway of an old building in Baku. Azeri, the Turkic language spoken in Azerbaijan, originally was written in Arabic. In the 1930s, the Soviets forced Azeris to adopt the Russian Cyrillic alphabet. In independent Azerbaijan, the local language appears in the same Latin-based lettering used in neighboring Turkey.* (Right) *Well-wishers carry flowers at a wedding party in the capital.*

Wool rugs made in Baku are distinctive for their use of muted colors and for combining strands of silk or cotton to highlight the overall design.

people of modern Azerbaijan, is an eastern dialect of Turkish that has borrowed many Persian and Russian words. Speakers of Turkish and Azeri can easily communicate with one another.

Until the early 20th century, when Azerbaijan came under Soviet rule, Turkish and Persian were the country's major languages. Both were written in the Arabic script. To **Russify** the Azeri population, the Soviets made the Russian language—as well as Cyrillic, the Russian alphabet—the official modes of communication.

Russian remained the official language of Azerbaijan until 1989, when the people of Azerbaijan replaced Russian with Azeri. Russians, Armenians, and other citizens now must learn Azeri in school and must use it in business and government.

(Above) *The minaret (tower) of a mosque in Baku dates from the 11th century, when Islamic khans (princes) ruled Azerbaijan.* (Below) *Faithful Muslims (followers of Islam) gather inside a mosque to pray.*

• Religion •

Arab armies brought the Islamic faith to Azerbaijan in the 7th century A.D. Early in its history, Islam split into two branches, or sects. Most Azeris are members of the minority Shiite sect, which is also the main faith of people in Iran. The followers of Islam, called Muslims, are required to fulfill several obligations. Devout Muslims, for example, pray five times daily, make donations to the poor, and fast during the holy month of Ramadan.

Under Soviet rule, the Islamic religion was severely restricted, and mosques were closed. In schools, instructors taught Azeri children to reject Islamic traditions. Reading the Koran (the Islamic holy book) was forbidden. Since independence, the Azeri government has removed these religious restrictions.

Azerbaijan's Armenians belong to the Armenian Apostolic Church, a Christian sect that was founded in Armenia in the 4th century A.D. The church's rites resemble those of the Eastern Orthodox Church, to which Russians, Georgians, and other former Soviet peoples belong.

• Health and Education •

Beginning in the 1920s, when Azerbaijan came under Soviet rule, the government built new medical and educational facilities. Health-care services were free or quite cheap, and the cost of education was also borne by the Soviet state. Without the financial support of the Soviet government, independent Azerbaijan now bears the costs of these benefits.

Despite having a large number of doctors and other medical personnel, Azerbaijan lacks the money to maintain adequate health services. Supplies of medicines and medical equipment are decreasing, and most rural clinics are having difficulty providing care. In the early 1990s, Azerbaijan had a high infant mortality rate of 45 deaths in every 1,000 live births. Life expectancy was about 70 years of age, an average figure compared to other former Soviet republics.

When the Soviets took over in 1922, they turned the Azeri educational system away from religious instruction, which included the study of Arabic and the Koran. Instead, the Soviets emphasized reading and writing in the Cyrillic alphabet, and the use of Arabic declined. As a result, much of Azerbaijan's classical literature, which appears in Arabic, has become difficult for Azeri students to understand.

In independent Azerbaijan, teachers are once again including religion in the curriculum. Middle Eastern nations are importing Korans, and Iran has begun to send mullahs (Islamic teachers) to Azerbaijan to provide religious instruction.

Modern Azerbaijan has thousands of elementary and high schools. These institutions have helped to give the nation a high literacy rate. Azerbaijan has more than a dozen institutions of higher learning, including the Academy of Sciences and the University of Azerbaijan in Baku.

Azeris under the age of 15 make up about one-third of the total population of 7.1 million.

Although only 5 percent of Azeris are older than 65, some of the elderly live very long lives. This 151-year-old woman visits with her great-granddaughter while spinning yarn.

Young students accompany their teacher on a day trip to the historic sections of Baku.

CHAPTER TWO

Azerbaijan's Story

A zerbaijan's location has played a major role in its history. For many centuries, the only way to travel from the Middle East, which is south and west of Azerbaijan, to Russia and other areas north of the Caucasus Mountains was through Azerbaijan along the Caspian Sea. Throughout the country's history, many nations have tried to control this vital passageway.

· Early Times ·

Archaeological remains indicate that people lived in Azerbaijan at least 6,000 years ago and probably as early as 25,000 years ago. Among the country's first permanent settlers were Caucasic

Massive tombs and leaning headstones dot an old cemetery in Shemakha, the former capital of the Shirvan khanate (realm of a khan). Destroyed in battle in 1742, the city was further damaged after an earthquake in the early 1900s.

peoples who came from various parts of the Caucasus Mountains. Another group, the Scythians, were
a semi-nomadic people who roamed the Black Sea
region before eventually settling in northeastern
Azerbaijan and southern Dagestan around the 9th
century B.C.

At about the same time, the Caucasic groups
had come in contact with the Medes, a people from
the south who were related to the Persians. In the
8th century B.C., the Medes established a strong
empire that covered northern Iran and southern
Azerbaijan. A rival Persian group, the Achaemenids,
fought for control of Median territory in the 6th century B.C. Under their leader Cyrus the Great, the
Achaemenids had taken over Azerbaijan and large
portions of the surrounding area by 550 B.C.

Cyrus was the first king of the Achaemenid
dynasty (family of rulers). He and his successors

*Early residents of Azerbaijan
followed a one-god religion
called Zoroastrianism whose
priests used fire in their cere-
monies. In Baku, fires are lit in
the Temple of the Firewor-
shipers.*

A mosaic shows the Greek leader Alexander the Great in battle. One of his generals conquered Azerbaijan in the early 4th century B.C. *After taking over the region, the general became known as Atropates, which means "protected by fire" in Greek. Alexander named the conquered area Media Atropatene, and the modern nation of Azerbaijan takes its name from various versions of this ancient Greek word.*

were strict rulers but wisely realized that centralized control would not work in such a vast empire. Instead, the Achaemenids set up **satrapies** that allowed a measure of self-rule to their domains. A governor, called a **satrap**, ruled these provinces with the help of an Achaemenid general who kept order and an Achaemenid secretary who kept records of trade and taxes.

The satrapy system worked well until the arrival of the Greek king Alexander the Great. In the early 4th century B.C., Alexander assembled an army and invaded the Achaemenid Empire. Alexander conquered the Achaemenid realm and eventually absorbed southern Azerbaijan, which he called **Media Atropatene.**

Alexander's purpose was to mix the cultures of Greece and Persia to fashion a strong superpower.

Alexander's early death in 323 B.C., however, left this dream unfinished. His generals divided his empire, with Azerbaijan becoming part of the domain of Seleucus.

• Foreign Rulers •

The Seleucid dynasty soon faced a strong challenge. The Roman Empire, which was centered in southern Europe on the Italian Peninsula, was expanding into the Seleucid state. By the 1st century A.D., the Romans had succeeded in **annexing** southern Azerbaijan, as well as northern Azerbaijan, which had remained in the hands of the Scythians. Although they were fierce warriors, the Scythians fought against Roman rule with little success. The Romans, after adding the Scythian realm to their empire, called the region **Albania.**

By the 3rd century A.D., internal rivalries were weakening Rome's hold on its vast territories. At this time, the Sasanians, a group related to the Persians, ruled Persia. Under the Sasanians, Persia reestablished control over southwestern Asia and Azerbaijan in the 4th century A.D.

Sasanian control lasted until A.D. 642, when Arab armies of Muslims—followers of a new faith called Islam—conquered the region. Islam, which originated in the Middle East, encouraged its believers to bring the faith to conquered peoples. During the 7th century A.D., Persia and Azerbaijan adopted Islam.

The Muslims left control largely in the hands of local elites. These powerful leaders eventually came to be called **khans,** and their domains were known as **khanates.** Within Azerbaijan, khanates were established around the cities of Shemakha in east central Azerbaijan, Kuba in the north central part of the country, and Nukha (now Sheki) in the north.

The poet Nezami, who was born in Gyanja in about 1141, is depicted in a modern portrait. His long, narrative works—including **Khamseh (The Quintuplet),** *a collection of five epic poems—are famous throughout southwestern Asia and have been translated into many languages.*

The Momine-Khatun Mausoleum (above-ground tomb) in Nakhichevan was built in about 1186, when the area was under the control of the Seljuk Turks. The top of the 10-sided structure carries inscriptions in the ancient Kufic (Arabic) script, as well as geometric designs made of glazed turquoise bricks.

From the 8th to the 11th centuries, these realms prospered. Cities in northern Azerbaijan became famous for ceramics, metalworking (especially copper and silver), woodcarving, leather goods, and the making of fine carpets. Shemakha, Kuba, and Nukha were all major centers of trade. Gyanja in western Azerbaijan also became a great commercial hub.

While Azerbaijan was prospering, a new group of immigrants—Seljuk Turks from central Asia—arrived in the region. They also followed the Islamic faith and organized their domains under khans. In addition, the Seljuks were fierce fighters commanded by skilled generals.

In the mid-11th century, a Seljuk khan named Toghril Beg sacked Baghdad, the center of the Islamic Empire, and forced its ruler to name him leader of the region that included Azerbaijan.

A miniature painting shows the Mongol warrior Hulegu Khan surrounded by his advisers and military commanders. Mongol forces captured the lands of Azerbaijan in the 13th century.

As a result of this move, Arab governmental control of the area ended. The Turkish language was introduced, and the local people intermarried with the Seljuks, causing the ethnic makeup and language of Azerbaijan to be slowly Turkized.

• New Invasions •

The Seljuks eventually expanded into Turkey, and this growth left their empire's Caucasus region vulnerable to invasions from central Asia. In the 13th century, armies of central Asian Mongols attacked Azerbaijan. Under their leader Hulegu Khan, the Mongols conquered the area and set up their capital at Tabriz in what is now northwestern Iran. From Tabriz, the Mongols ruled Azerbaijan and Persia, both of which became major centers of learning and trade in the 14th century.

Beginning in the 1700s, the town of Sheki (ancient Nukha) was the site of a khan's palace, whose interior was richly decorated.

Weak rulers caused Mongol control to fall apart in the early 1400s, permitting Turkish groups in the region to establish short-lived, independent realms. The Al-Qoyunlu and Kara Qoyunlu were Muslims who held sway in Azerbaijan and northern Iran for more than a century. After seizing Tabriz, these groups spent decades fending off attacks from Turkey.

By the early 16th century, another dynasty—the Safavids of Azerbaijan—had taken over Persia, establishing a strong realm with its capital at Qazvin in northern Iran. The Safavids expanded trade and renewed Azerbaijan's prosperity, especially at Shemakha.

Meanwhile, the Ottoman Turks had replaced the Seljuks in Turkey. In the 18th century, the Ottoman Turks and the Safavid Persians frequently fought for control of Azerbaijan, which lay along

Throughout the 18th and 19th centuries, Persian and Ottoman Turkish armies battled for control of Azerbaijan. A painting in the khan's palace at Sheki depicts a Persian general and his army on the march.

important trade routes. Another force, the power-ful Russian Empire to the north of Azerbaijan, also began to encroach on Azeri lands. Throughout the 18th century, however, the Safavids retained control of the region.

In the early 19th century, Russian military victories forced Persia to give up the territory that became the modern Republic of Azerbaijan. Russia seized the cities of Baku, Nukha, Shemakha, Gyanja, and Lenkoran, as well as the ancient trade routes that went through these urban centers. These takeovers were recognized by the Treaty of Gulistan in 1813. As the result of another war and treaty between Russia and Persia, Russia annexed Nakhichevan and the southern part of Talysh in 1828.

• Decades of Change •

The Christian Russians, who had also invaded the lands of the Christian Armenians, allowed a great immigration of Armenians into Azerbaijan. Some came as refugees from the wars in Turkey and Persia. Others were skilled traders, educators, and craftspeople who played important roles in Azerbaijan's economic development.

Most Armenians settled in and around Azerbaijan's major cities. Azeris, however, saw the Armenians as anti-Muslim and anti-Azeri and resented the large Armenian populations in Azeri urban areas. In addition, the Russian government favored the Armenians over the Azeris—a policy that worsened tensions between the two groups.

In the mid-1800s, the discovery of oil in the Caspian Sea encouraged the Russians to develop the economy of Azerbaijan. By the late 19th century, Baku had become the world's largest supplier of petroleum. As a result, building flourished in the capital, which became one of the region's major

As Persia and Turkey continued to fight over the Caucasus region, another power—the Russian Empire—began to push southward into the same area. This map shows the Russian annexations of territory that took place in the 1800s.

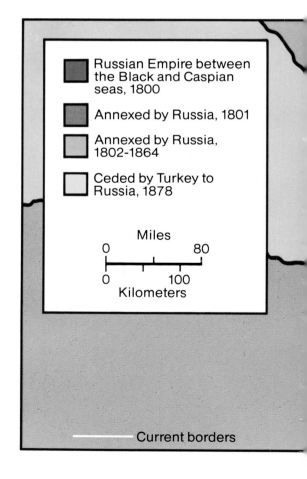

Russian Empire between the Black and Caspian seas, 1800

Annexed by Russia, 1801

Annexed by Russia, 1802-1864

Ceded by Turkey to Russia, 1878

Miles
0   80

0   100
Kilometers

—— Current borders

ports. Workers laid railway lines that linked Baku with Batumi, a Georgian port on the Black Sea. Foreign companies hastened to Azerbaijan to make money from oil.

By the early 20th century, many groups in the Russian Empire were working toward self-rule. The Azeris, who felt that the revenues from oil were benefiting only Russians and other foreigners, looked for help from Muslim Turkey and Muslim Persia. In 1911, Azeri intellectuals formed the nationalist Musavat (Equality) party. Their aim was to unite Muslim states in the region and to liberate them from foreign domination.

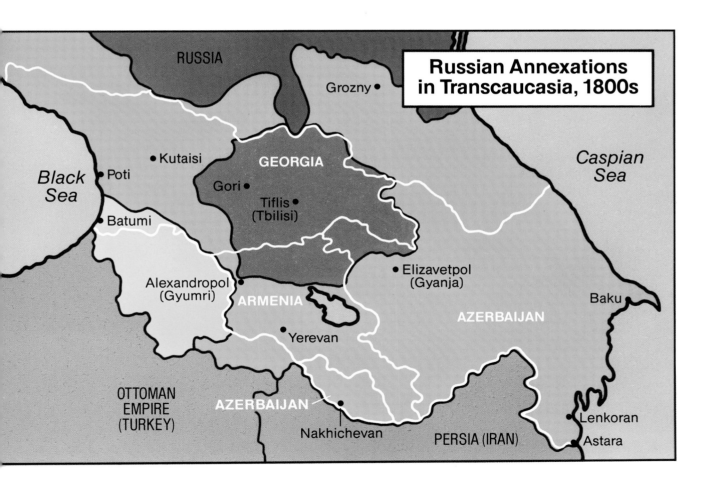

In 1918 – during fighting between Azeris and Communist forces – the bodies of dead people and horses littered a street in Baku. Also involved in the conflict were Turkish troops and the British army, both of which were trying to take Azerbaijan out of Russian control.

These plans were interrupted in 1914, when Russia became involved in World War I. This international conflict pitted Russia, France, and Britain against Germany and Ottoman Turkey. Russian military defeats and mismanagement led to great hardships and political turmoil. Many people began to support the views of revolutionaries called Communists, who were promising peace, food, and land. By late 1917, the Communists had succeeded in overthrowing the Russian government.

The loss of central control threw the Russian Empire into chaos. Armenians and Azeris fought one another, and both sides committed massacres. Meanwhile, the Communists occupied Baku in an attempt to oust the Musavat party and to seize Azeri lands. Eventually, Azeri leaders put aside their differences long enough to declare Azerbaijan's independence in 1918. The new republic won international recognition in 1920. Within months, however, the powerful Communist Red Army had invaded, and the Azeri government surrendered.

Azeris leave flowers at a Baku monument that is dedicated to 26 Communist leaders whom the British executed in 1918.

• *Soviet Rule* •

In 1922, the Communists combined Azerbaijan, Armenia, and Georgia into the Transcaucasian Soviet Federated Socialist Republic. This federation was a member of the newly formed Union of Soviet Socialist Republics (USSR). Under a constitutional reform passed in 1936, the three republics became separate members of the Soviet Union.

Under Soviet rule, the central government in Moscow (the capital of the USSR) set Azerbaijan's economic, social, cultural, and political policies. In the 1930s, the Soviet government took over Azerbaijan's industries—including its valuable oil industry. Workers left local trades to labor in large, Soviet-sponsored factories that refined oil and manufactured petrochemicals. Thousands of people came to Baku and Sumgait in search of jobs.

Soviet leaders also forcibly combined Azeri farms into huge estates as part of the **collective-farm program.** In the past, Azeri farmers had raised food for their own tables and to sell in local markets. The Soviets now ordered these farmers to grow cotton—the raw material for Soviet textile mills. Azeri farmers who fought against collectivization were sent to prison or killed.

As these changes were occurring in Azerbaijan, events in Europe were leading to World War II (1939–1945). Although much of the western USSR was destroyed in this conflict, Azerbaijan and other areas of Transcaucasia escaped damage. The Red Army, however, invaded Iran in 1941 to put Azeri lands in both countries under Soviet control. Postwar treaties forced the Soviets to return these newly annexed lands to Iran.

After the war, the Soviet Union expanded the petroleum industry in Azerbaijan to include the manufacture of oil equipment. The vast oil fields of Russia, developed in the 1950s and 1960s, came to depend on Azeri-built petroleum machinery. Oil wells near Baku continued to pump oil, which a pipeline transported to Batumi in Georgia.

• Recent Events •

This growth overshadowed the ethnic hatreds within Azerbaijan. For the most part, the USSR's control over information and politics prevented violence between Azeris and Armenians. In the late 1980s, however, the new Soviet leader Mikhail Gorbachev introduced **glasnost**, a policy of open dialogue that allowed peoples throughout the USSR to express their views without fear of punishment.

Glasnost made it possible for the Azerbaijan Popular Front to form and to press for independence. The ethnic divisions that had been suppressed for decades surfaced in 1988, as Azeris and Armenians fought one another in Sumgait. The violence eventually spread to Nagorno-Karabakh, the mostly Armenian **enclave** in central Azerbaijan. Fighting also broke out along Nakhichevan's border with Armenia.

Gorbachev tried to stop the conflict through diplomacy but finally ordered Soviet troops to occupy Baku. For conservative leaders in Moscow, the ethnic unrest showed that Gorbachev's policies were giving the USSR's many nationalities too much freedom. Fearing a loss of centralized control, these conservative Communists staged a **coup d'état** (sudden overthrow) of Gorbachev in August 1991. The coup failed and left the Soviet government too weak to stop the withdrawal of republics from the union. Spurred by the Popular Front, Azerbaijan's president Ayaz Mutalibov declared his country's independence in early September 1991.

Gaining independence has done little to lessen the conflicts in the region. In Nagorno-Karabakh,

In September 1991, ethnic Azeris raised their country's new flag during a Popular Front demonstration for independence. The emblem carries the star and crescent—symbols of the Islamic religion.

One of the most pressing challenges to the stability of independent Azerbaijan is the ethnic conflict in Nagorno-Karabakh. Here, a wounded woman is helped to an aid station after a shelling attack in Stepanakert.

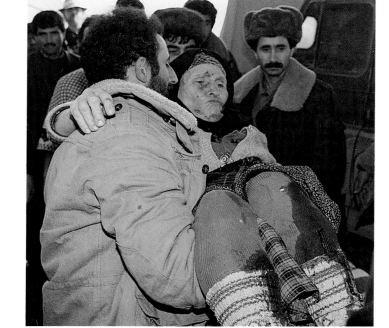

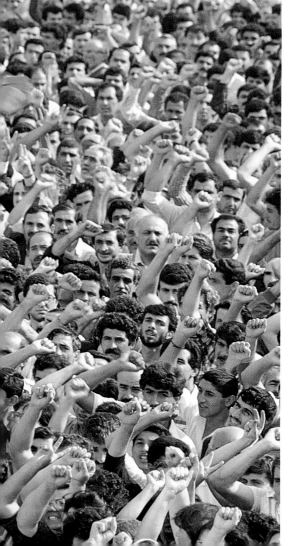

Armenians are determined either to have self-rule or to join their land with Armenia. Similarly, Azeris in Nakhichevan have destroyed barricades on the border with northwestern Iran to express their desire to reunite with Azeris there.

Demonstrations forced Mutalibov to resign in March 1992, but he was back in power in May. Within a few days, a coup had swept him from office again and had installed new leaders from the Popular Front. Elections in June confirmed Ebulfez Elcibey, the candidate of the Popular Front, as president.

Although Azerbaijan has a well-developed industrial and agricultural base, the country's economic prospects depend on peace and political stabililty. It remains to be seen whether the new Azeri government, which may be dominated by anti-Armenian factions, can bring the stability and growth that Azerbaijan needs to survive and prosper.

CHAPTER THREE

Making a Living in Azerbaijan

Soviet rule brought Azerbaijan industrial and agricultural development, as well as governmental corruption, environmental abuse, and economic inefficiency. To transform the complex economy inherited from the Soviet era will take time. The new Azeri government wants to turn over some state-owned farms and businesses to private citizens. It also plans to introduce a new currency—the Azeri manat—in the near future. All of these changes however, depend on political stability. War with Armenia may delay or prevent Azerbaijan's economic recovery.

One area of success has been Azerbaijan's ability to forge new commercial ties in the region.

Carrying their shovels over their shoulders, workers walk to their jobs.

The Soviet Union's control of Azerbaijan's economy extended even to the imagery chosen for the country's famous carpets. Here, a man poses beneath a rug that depicts Vladimir Lenin, the founder of the Soviet Union.

Although much of Azerbaijan's trade still occurs with Russia and with other former Soviet republics, Azeri leaders joined a new Islamic economic association in mid-1992. The union includes Turkey, Iran, Pakistan, as well as the former Soviet central Asian republics of Uzbekistan, Kyrgyzstan, Tajikistan, and Turkmenistan.

A crew of workers picks tea leaves on a farming estate near Lenkoran.

Not far from Gyanja, laborers (above) **gather hay. A farmer** (below) **struggles to fix his pea-harvesting machine.**

• *Agriculture* •

Although Azerbaijan earns substantial export income from agriculture, only about one-seventh of the country is under cultivation. Throughout the Kura lowlands, farming is possible with extensive irrigation. In the foothills of the mountains, rainfall is plentiful enough for crops to flourish without extra watering. Some agricultural practices, however, have led to soil erosion and soil infertility—problems Azeri farmers will have to face in the near future.

In the 1920s, when Azerbaijan joined the USSR, the Soviet government forced the new republic to switch from the raising of traditional foods to the cultivation of specialized crops that did not grow in most of the Soviet Union. Azeri farmers now harvest high-quality grapes, apricots, peaches, pears, apples, pomegranates, and melons in a subtropical region near Lenkoran. Grapes also grow in Nakhichevan, Nagorno-Karabakh, and northern Azerbaijan. Tea is an important crop in the Talysh Mountains.

PLANES SPRAY PESTICIDES (INSECT-KILLING CHEMICALS) ON CROPS

LIVESTOCK GRAZE ON PLANTS CONTAINING PESTICIDES AND TAKE IN THE CHEMICALS

PESTICIDE OVERKILL IN AZERBAIJAN

In 1960, farmers in the Soviet Union began to spray and dump huge amounts of **pesticides** on their fields to rid cotton, vegetables, and fruits of crop-destroying pests. This practice continued for three decades and had spread throughout the USSR by 1990. Azerbaijan, the leading producer of cotton in the Caucasus region, still pours more pesticides on its farmland than any other former Soviet republic.

Pesticides are chemicals that control or kill bugs, rodents, and bacteria (tiny life forms), which can harm crops and reduce harvests. But pesticides also hurt animals, including humans. Rain or irrigation water can carry these chemicals into the soil of surrounding pastures and into rivers and lakes. Animals that feed on the contaminated plants or live in the polluted waters absorb the pesticides. When humans eat these ani-

PEOPLE CONSUME PESTICIDES BY EATING
PLANTS AND ANIMALS THAT HAVE THE
CHEMICALS IN THEIR TISSUES

FISH AND BIRDS
ABSORB PESTICIDES
IN THE POLLUTED
WATER

PESTICIDES FILTER THROUGH THE SOIL TO
UNDERGROUND WATER SOURCES THAT LEAD
TO RIVERS AND LAKES

mals, they also take in the poisonous chemicals.

For more than three decades, Azerbaijan has sprayed DDT, one of the most deadly pesticides, on its crops. DDT dries slowly but is quickly absorbed into the tissues of animals, plants, and people. More than 20 years ago, most countries —including the Soviet Union—officially banned DDT, but Azeri farmers continue to use the pesticide in strong doses.

Scientists in Azerbaijan have recognized the unhealthy effects of pesticides and have set up new methods of pest control. The most common alternative to pesticides is the introduction of harmless bugs that do not feed on crops but rather eat crop-destroying insects. This approach, as well as other non-chemical means, may soon rid Azerbaijan's farms of harmful pesticides while protecting crops from unwanted insects.

Azerbaijan is a major producer of cotton, especially in Nakhichevan and in central Azerbaijan. The crop supplies the country's textile factories. Greenhouses around Baku specialize in the growing of fresh flowers, and farmers raise tobacco and silkworms near Lenkoran. For local markets, Azeris plant wheat, barley, hardy vegetables, herbs, and potatoes in southern and western Azerbaijan.

In the mountain regions of Azerbaijan, most people make their living by raising sheep and goats. Cattle are also found in large numbers throughout the country. Nutritious grasses for livestock grow well in Nagorno-Karabakh, as well as in northern, south central, and eastern Azerbaijan. In addition to meat, Azeri herds provide wool, hides, milk, and cheese.

Herding sheep or goats is a common job among Azeris who live in the mountains.

A team of harvesters makes its way through a vast field of ripening cotton, which is Azerbaijan's leading agricultural product. Raw cotton supplies Azeri textile mills and is still exported to the former Soviet republics.

Azeris weld pipes for use in the deep-sea oil stations near Baku.

At a building site near Len-koran, a truck unloads bricks made in the region's factories from local materials.

• Manufacturing •

Azerbaijan's oil resources led to the development of a large-scale petrochemical industry, whose revenues now go to the Azeri republic instead of to Moscow. On the Apsheron Peninsula, oil refineries, petroleum industries, plants that make plastics and synthetics, and a modern chemical industry are the major employers. The peninsula also is the most important producer of equipment for the petroleum and natural-gas industries of the former USSR.

Other products manufactured in Azerbaijan include textiles and lightweight industrial goods that come from factories in Baku, Gyanja, Sheki, Mingechaur, Stepanakert, and Nakhichevan. The cotton industry thrives in the Kura lowlands. Workers make building materials at plants in Lenkoran, Karadag, and Nakhichevan. The port of Baku on the Caspian Sea has become an important shipbuilding hub.

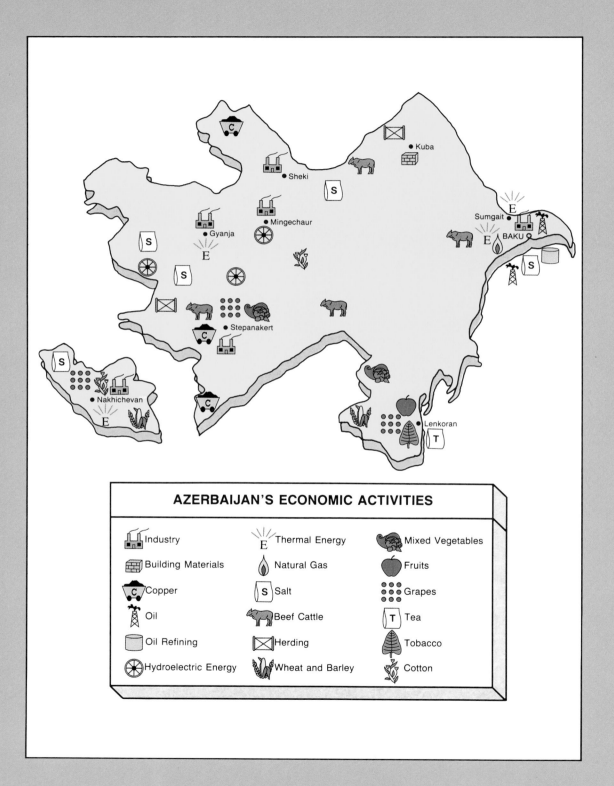

AZERBAIJAN'S ECONOMIC ACTIVITIES

Industry
Thermal Energy
Mixed Vegetables

Building Materials
Natural Gas
Fruits

Copper
Salt
Grapes

Oil
Beef Cattle
Tea

Oil Refining
Herding
Tobacco

Hydroelectric Energy
Wheat and Barley
Cotton

• Mining and Energy •

Although mining is not a major source of income in Azerbaijan, the country has deposits of several valuable minerals. Zinc, copper, and salt come from central, northern, and southern parts of Azerbaijan. Baku and western Azerbaijan are major suppliers of salt. Building stone is a principal product from Kuba, and copper and sulfur deposits lie in the east and center of the nation.

For energy, Azerbaijan relies on its own oil reserves, which have been declining in volume since the 1940s. Nevertheless, oil and oil refining are still major industries on the Apsheron Peninsula. The Soviets built a pipeline to carry refined oil from Baku to Batumi. Other pipelines transport natural gas from Karadag to Akstafa in Azerbaijan and to Tbilisi in Georgia. The ethnic conflicts in the region have stopped shipments of gas to Armenia.

Azeri factories also tap energy created by thermal plants near Nakhichevan, Gyanja, Sumgait, and Baku that use heat to make electricity. Hydroelectric stations generate power on the Kura River in Mingechaur, as well as at plants in Dashkesan and in central Azerbaijan.

An oil worker (above) *rests beneath drilling equipment on the Apsheron Peninsula. A line of drilling platforms* (below) *stretches into the Caspian Sea.*

CHAPTER FOUR

What's Next for Azerbaijan?

T he Azeri government has recognized the environmental, cultural, and political problems inherited from the Communist system. The Azeri people see the new Russian government as pro-Armenian and anti-Azeri. As a result, many Azeris have become anti-Soviet, anti-Communist, and even anti-Russian.

This attitude caused Azerbaijan to be one of the last republics of the former Soviet Union to join the **Commonwealth of Independent States.** Founded in late 1991, this economic and military association has become disunified. Many Azeris—especially those who hoped the commonwealth would stop the conflict in Nagorno-Karabakh—are pressing for Azerbaijan to withdraw from the union.

Vendors chat and arrange their goods at a farmer's market in Gyanja.

Warfare continues to rage between ethnic Armenians and ethnic Azeris over control of Nagorno-Karabakh. Thousands of people have been killed on both sides. A blockade imposed by Azeri workers on goods traveling to Armenia and to Nagorno-Karabakh has hampered trade in the region. Although the loss of trade has hurt Azerbaijan, the ongoing war with Armenia is even more damaging.

An Azeri homeowner sits amid the rubble of his house after a bombing attack in Nagorno-Karabakh.

FAST FACTS ABOUT AZERBAIJAN

Total Population	7.1 million
Ethnic Mixture	85 percent Azeri 6 percent Russian 6 percent Armenian
CAPITAL and Major Cities	BAKU, Gyanja Sumgait, Lenkoran
Major Language	Azeri Turkish
Major Religion	Islam (Shiite branch)
Year of inclusion in USSR	1922
Status	Independent state; member of United Nations since 1992; conflicts with Armenia over status of Nagorno-Karabakh and Nakhichevan

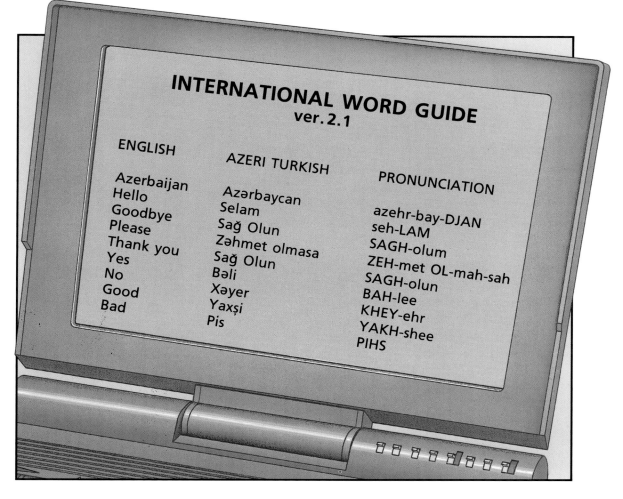

INTERNATIONAL WORD GUIDE
ver. 2.1

ENGLISH	AZERI TURKISH	PRONUNCIATION
Azerbaijan	Azərbaycan	azehr-bay-DJAN
Hello	Selam	seh-LAM
Goodbye	Sağ Olun	SAGH-olum
Please	Zəhmet olmasa	ZEH-met OL-mah-sah
Thank you	Sağ Olun	SAGH-olun
Yes	Bəli	BAH-lee
No	Xəyer	KHEY-ehr
Good	Yaxşi	YAKH-shee
Bad	Pis	PIHS

Azerbaijan is looking to the Middle East for new alliances and perhaps for military help in its struggle against the Armenians. Many Azeris want to reunite their country with Iran's Azeri community. Other Azeris are pushing for closer ties with Turkey.

For the first time, Azeris have been able to elect their leaders freely, and political disagreement does not result in punishment. In March 1992, the **United Nations** recognized Azerbaijan's independence and invited the country to join its ranks. Despite these positive signs of growth and acceptance, Azerbaijan must resolve its conflicts with Armenia before real progress can take place.

Albania: the name the ancient Romans gave to a country on the western shores of the Caspian Sea inhabited by the Scythians.

annex: to add a country or territory to the domain of another by force.

collective-farm program: a system of large agricultural estates worked by a group. The workers usually received a portion of the farm's harvest as wages. On a Soviet collective farm, the central government owned the land, buildings, and machinery.

Commonwealth of Independent States: a union of former Soviet republics that was created by the leaders of Russia, Belarus, and Ukraine in December 1991. The commonwealth has no formal constitution and functions as a loose economic and military association.

Communist: a person who supports Communism—an economic system in which the government owns all farmland and the means of producing goods in factories.

coup d'état: French words meaning "blow to the state" that refer to a swift, sudden overthrow of a government.

enclave: an area that is culturally distinct but that lies entirely within a foreign country.

ethnic Armenian: a person who speaks Armenian and whose ancestors came from the territory of **historic Armenia.**

ethnic Azeri: a person whose ethnic heritage is Turkic and who speaks Azeri.

ethnic Russian: a person whose ethnic heritage is Slavic and who speaks Russian.

glasnost: the Russian word for openness that refers to a Soviet policy of easing restrictions on writing and speech.

In Baku, a merchant offers fresh watermelons for sale.

historic Armenia: a large area of southwestern Asia—including parts of modern Turkey, Iran, Armenia, Georgia, and Azerbaijan—that was frequently under Armenian authority between the 2nd century B.C. and the 11th century A.D.

industrialize: to build and modernize factories for the purpose of manufacturing a wide variety of consumer goods and machinery.

khan: the leader of a central Asian domain, called a **khanate,** who ruled Turkic, Mongol, or Tatar peoples.

During the Soviet era, Azeris demonstrated in the capital in front of the headquarters of the Communist party.

Azeri artisans crafted the wooden and stone decorations on this doorway in old Baku.

Media Atropatene: the name Alexander the Great gave to an area of southwestern Asia, including Azerbaijan, in the 4th century B.C.

pesticide: a chemical used to destroy insects or other pests.

Russian Empire: a large kingdom ruled by czars that covered present-day Russia as well as areas to the west and south. It existed from roughly the mid-1500s to 1917.

Russify: to make Russian by imposing the Russian language and culture on non-Russian peoples.

satrap: the governor of a region, called a **satrapy**, in the ancient Achaemenid Empire (now in modern Iran).

Transcaucasian republic: one of the three southwest Asian republics of Azerbaijan, Armenia, and Georgia that were once part of the USSR and that have the Caucasus Mountains crossing their territories.

Turkization: to make Turkic by introducing the Turkic language and culture to non-Turkic peoples.

Union of Soviet Socialist Republics (USSR): a large nation in eastern Europe and northern Asia that consisted of 15 member-republics. It existed from 1922 to 1991.

United Nations: an international organization formed after World War II whose primary purpose is to promote world peace through discussion and cooperation.

An Azeri weaver pauses in front of her loom.

• *Photo Acknowledgments* •

Photographs are used courtesy of: pp. 1, 2, 5, 9, 13, 17, 18 (bottom), 22, 24, 28, 41 (top and bottom), 44 (top), 45 (left), 48, © Yury Tatarinov; pp. 6, 12 (top and bottom), 23 (top), 36, 37, 40 (right), 44 (bottom), 45 (right), 50 (right), TASS / SOVFOTO; pp. 8 (left and right), 18 (top), 19, 20, 31 (top), 55, Ron Wixman; pp. 10, 16 (bottom), 21 (bottom), 38, 40 (left), 47 (bottom), © George Steinmetz; pp. 16 (top), 26, 29, 31 (bottom), © Emile S. / The Hutchison Library; pp. 21 (top), 34 (right), 52, © Eugene G. Schulz; p. 23 (bottom), © J. Brugmann / AMSTOCK; p. 27, Independent Picture Service; p. 30, Culture and Tourism Office of the Turkish Embassy; p. 34 (left), UPI / Bettmann; pp. 47 (top), 53, Aramco World; p. 54, Sergej Schachowskoj. Maps and charts: pp. 14–15, 46, J. Michael Roy; pp. 32–33, 50, 51, Laura Westlund; pp. 42–43, Bryan Liedahl.

Covers: (Front and Back) © Yury Tatarinov